Food
& You

Eating Right, Being Strong, and Feeling Great

by Dr. Lynda Madison

★ American Girl®

Published by American Girl Publishing, Inc.

Questions or comments? Call 1-800-845-0005, visit our Web site at **americangirl.com**, or write to Customer Service, American Girl, 8400 Fairway Place, Middleton, WI 53562-0497.

Dr. Lynda Madison is a licensed psychologist and a nationally recognized speaker on the topics of adolescent girls, eating disorders, and family relationships. She is associate director of Foccus Inc., U.S.A., and associate professor at Creighton University School of Medicine.

Printed in China

08 09 10 11 12 13 14 LEO 10 9 8 7 6 5 4 3 2 1

All American Girl marks are trademarks of American Girl, LLC.

Editorial Development: Erin Falligant, Michelle Watkins

Art Direction & Design: Chris Lorette David, Valerie Pulvermacher

Cover: Photography, Jose Martinez; Direction, Julie Mierkiewicz

Model Photography page 12: John McArthur

Production: Jeannette Bailey, Judith Lary, Julie Kimmell, Gretchen Krause, and Gail Longworth

Special thanks to Georgia Walter, Registered Dietician

This book is not intended to replace the advice of or treatment by physicians. Questions or concerns about physical health should always be discussed with a doctor, dietician, or other health-care provider.

Cataloging-in-Publication Data available from the Library of Congress.

Dear Reader,

You get a lot of messages about food and weight from TV, magazines, and the people around you. There's so much talk that it's hard to know what—and how—to eat. How can you cut through the confusion?

First, go to the right sources—your parents, your doctor, and books like this. Don't pay too much attention to ads you see in magazines or on TV.

Second, trust your body. It'll tell you when it's hungry or happy, such as after exercise or a healthy meal.

Third, have fun! There are so many healthy foods that taste great. If you haven't found them yet, keep looking. And try the suggestions in this book sent in by girls like you.

When you give your body what it needs, it'll give you what you need—energy, a clear head at school, and the confidence to be your own girl.

Your friends at American Girl

Contents

Food & You

Just the Facts

Meals & Snacks

On the Move

Help! Q&A

Confused by messages that tell you to change what you eat or how you look? Here's what you need to know.

7 Big Truths

1. There are no bad foods.

You can eat a *little* of any food and still be healthy. Just try to reach for nutritious foods first. Junk food, such as cookies and chips, can be high in sugar, salt, and artificial colors and flavors (junk!). If you eat too much of it, you won't have room for what your body really needs.

2. What you drink counts.

You need at least five 8-ounce glasses of water a day. When you exercise, you need even more water. You can get some from milk, which is great for bones and teeth. But go easy on soda and fruit drinks, which may contain caffeine or sugar. They'll give you a quick burst of energy but then leave you feeling tired.

3. Your waist and weight will change as you grow.

As your body develops, your waist will grow along with the rest of you, and your clothes will fit more tightly. This is completely normal. You need to gain weight in order to grow. As you get taller, your weight is likely to even out. Your doctor can tell you if your weight is healthy for your height.

4. No body is perfect.

Don't believe what you see in magazines. Most photos are touched up to make models look thinner or shapelier than they really are. If you want to see real bodies, look around you. Some are tall, and some are short. Some are straight, and some are curvy. Basic body shape is something you're born with, and no one shape is better than another.

5. Crash diets don't work!

Diets that promise to help you lose weight *fast* won't work in the long run. If you cut down too much on what you eat, your body will try to protect itself. Your *metabolism* will slow down, which means your body won't use the calories in food as quickly and might store them as fat.

6. Staying active is a smart(er) move.

Exercise helps you stay at a healthy weight. How? By burning calories and building muscle, which boosts your metabolism. Challenging your body gives your self-esteem a boost, too. For a happier, healthier you, get up and get moving for at least an hour a day.

7. Food is a family thing.

When it comes to caring for your body, your parents are your best partners. Let them know if you want to make changes to your diet. Go shopping and plan a few dinners together. Try new foods that your parents make for you. Make dates to eat meals together—even during busy times.

Take a peek at the food pyramid, and find out which foods are doing the most for your body. How do your favorite foods stack up?

The Pyramid

Take the Test

Cover your eyes and see if you can name all the food groups. How'd you do? This pyramid shows a healthy mix of food for a 10-year-old girl who gets 30 to 60 minutes of exercise a day. To create your own pyramid, go to www.mypyramid.gov.

How Much Is Enough?

You don't need measuring cups or a scale to get the nutrition you need. Just keep these guidelines in mind:

Grains

An ounce equals a slice of bread or a bowl of cereal. You need about 6 ounces each day.

Vegetables

A cup is a scoop of vegetables about the size of a tennis ball. You need 2½ cups a day.

Grains

Vegetables

Pack your meals and snacks with foods from all the food groups in the pyramid.

Fruits
A cup equals an apple the size of a fist. You need 1½ cups a day.

Milk/Dairy
A cup is a medium-sized (8-ounce) glass of milk or a piece of cheese as big as a Ping-Pong ball. You need 3 cups a day.

Meats and Beans (and Eggs and Nuts)
An ounce is one egg or a tablespoonful of peanut butter. A piece of meat the size of a deck of cards equals 2½ ounces, or half of what you need each day.

Fats and Oils
You need about 5 teaspoons, or a handful of nuts, a day.

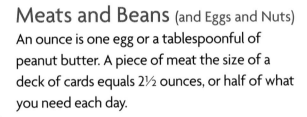

Fruits

Fats and Oils

Milk/Dairy

Meats and Beans

Nutrient News

Carbohydrates
Turn to carbohydrates when you need a boost of energy. Carbs are found in most foods, but the best sources are grains, fruits, and vegetables.

Proteins
Want to build muscle? Reach for meat, milk, nuts, eggs, and beans. Some girls are *vegetarians*, which means they don't eat meat. You can get protein from other foods, but it's tricky. Talk to a doctor or dietician before giving up meat.

Vitamins
Vitamins A, B, C, E, and K keep your eyes, skin, and blood healthy. You can find them in fruits and vegetables. Vitamin D helps you form strong teeth and bones. Get your D from milk, eggs, and fish. To make sure you get the vitamins you need, eat a variety of food.

Minerals

Calcium helps you build strong bones and teeth. You can get it from milk products and dark green vegetables. Iron keeps your blood healthy, and you'll find it in meat, beans, whole grains, and dried fruits.

Fats

Fat helps you build healthy cells and absorb vitamins. Nuts, avocados, salmon, and olive oil have omega-3 fatty acids, which are good for your body. Steer clear of saturated fat and trans-fatty acids, which aren't very healthy. They're found in butter, ice cream, French fries, and some crackers and cookies.

Fiber

Fiber keeps food moving through your digestive system and carries waste out. To fill up on fiber, eat vegetables, fruits, nuts, and whole grains.

Smart Choices

1. whole-wheat bread
or
white bread

2. light green lettuce
or
dark green lettuce

3. peanuts
or
potato chips

4. fruit
or
fruit juice

5. 2% milk
or
skim milk

Which of the two is better for you? Circle the healthier food or drink.

Answers:

1. **Whole-wheat.** Whole-grain foods have more fiber and nutrients. Look for foods that say "whole" before the name of the grain (such as "wheat" or "oats") on the label.

2. **The darker, the better.** All vegetables are good for you. But dark green or orange veggies, such as broccoli and carrots, have the most vitamins and minerals.

3. **Peanuts.** Both peanuts and potato chips have a lot of fat, but peanuts have the healthier kind of fat. And nuts are packed with protein.

4. **Whole fruit** is better than juice. Fruit has fiber, which fills you up and keeps your digestive system running well. Plus, fruit juices often contain extra sugars. Whole fruit is the naturally sweet choice.

5. **Skim milk** is fat-free, so it's healthier than whole, 2%, and 1% milk. Talk to your parents about switching to skim or 1%. Or make the change gradually from 2% to 1% and then to skim.

A Pretty Plate

Red
Apples, strawberries, watermelon, tomatoes, peppers

Orange
Carrots, sweet potatoes, oranges, apricots, cantaloupe

Yellow
Squash, sweet corn, wax beans, bananas, pineapple

What's the easiest way to get the vitamins you need? Dish up a rainbow of colorful foods.

Green
Peas, lettuce, broccoli, pears, honeydew melon

Blue and Purple
Blueberries, grapes, plums, raisins, purple (red) cabbage

Quiz
Your Eating Style

Which statements sound like you?

❑ I could win a blue ribbon in the "World's Slowest Eater" contest.

❑ The crumbs in the couch are mine—I eat while watching TV.

❑ Sometimes I eat my dinner standing up.

❑ I can polish off a whole box of snacks while I'm doing something else.

❑ I like to make my plate look pretty before I dig in for the first bite.

❑ I spend more time in the drive-through than at the dinner table.

❑ Sometimes I'm surprised to find my plate empty. Where'd all the food go?

❑ I often help my parents make recipes from scratch.

❑ Breakfast? Who has time for breakfast?

How you eat is just as important as what you eat.

If you answered mostly RED: You can do lots of things at once. But if you eat while you're distracted, you won't really enjoy your food and might eat more than you need. Instead of snacking while you watch TV or do homework, look for other things to do with your hands. Doodle on a pad of paper or squeeze a squishy ball.

If you answered mostly GREEN: You enjoy everything about food, from cooking it to savoring it at the table. Eating slowly is a good thing—it gives your brain time to know when you're full. Just try not to nibble too much before or after the meal. Chew gum while you cook, and help clean up the dishes as soon as you're done.

If you answered mostly BLUE: Whew! You're a busy girl. Try to make time for at least one sit-down meal a day. When you're on the go, don't grab salty, high-fat foods just because they're convenient. Pack healthy snacks in small bags that you can grab on your way out the door.

Meals & Snacks

Your body burns energy constantly, so refuel it throughout the day. Three meals and a couple of snacks will keep you going strong.

A Smart Start

The Facts

Compared to people who don't eat breakfast, breakfast eaters tend to . . .

- feel better,
- stay thinner,
- live longer,
- be healthier, and
- do better in school.

So when you get up, eat up!

Tasty Time-Savers

Don't have much time in the morning? Here are super-fast meals that give your body what it needs:

- whole-wheat toast with peanut butter and an orange
- yogurt with granola and strawberries
- instant oatmeal with raisins and a glass of milk
- a whole-grain bagel with low-fat cream cheese and an apple
- multigrain cereal topped with milk and blueberries
- cold pizza with whole-wheat crust and lots of veggies

In the Bag

Sandwiches and Spreads

Try a pita pocket instead of plain bread, or build your sandwich on a bagel. Roll up peanut butter, honey, and banana in a tortilla. Sandwich too dry? Butter and mayo add fat but little nutrition. Instead, try low-fat cream cheese and salsa, or a sweet combo of dried cranberries and yogurt.

Dippin' Veggies

Add crunch to your lunch with cut-up carrots, celery, or cucumbers. Fill a tiny tub with peanut butter, hummus, or salsa for dipping. On a chilly school day, tote veggie soup in a thermos.

Juicy Fruit

Toss in an apple, a banana, or some grapes. Fruit cups are handy but may be high in sugar. Fruit packed in unsweetened juice is best. Make your own combos, such as sliced strawberries and kiwi or peaches and blueberries.

Sweet and Salty Snacks

Pack a single serving of whole-wheat crackers, popcorn, or cereal. Or try a trail mix of nuts, raisins, and a few chocolate chips. Steer clear of snack machines at school—they're often stocked with high-fat, high-sugar foods.

Food Talk

If people make hurtful comments about your lunch or your eating, stay cool and try these comebacks. If someone says . . .

"What kind of diet are you on?" Say, "A normal, healthy diet. I eat some of almost everything."

"You're eating all that?" Say, "Sure! I can think better in school (or run harder in soccer) if I eat a good lunch."

Remember not to comment on your friends' eating habits, either. Every girl is in charge of her own body and what she puts into it.

29

Dinner In

Get Involved

Ask your parents if you can help plan a meal. Flip through books and magazines to find healthy recipes. Make a shopping list, and head to the store. Then hang out in the kitchen and help your parents make the meal. How does it taste? What can you do differently next time?

Experiment

Try out tasty toppings. Instead of creamy dressings and sauces, try lemon juice, yogurt, olive oil, or salsa.

Partner up with your parents to find foods you like and healthy ways to prepare them.

Be Sneaky

If you're not a vegetable lover, brainstorm ways to mix veggies into your meal. Can you simmer them in a soup or stew? Blend them into spaghetti sauce? Tuck them under the cheese on a pizza?

Sit and Savor

Ask your parents if you can plan a special dinner once a week. Dress up the table with a tablecloth or place mats. Fill a vase with flowers, or ask a parent to light a candle. Sit down and eat slowly, enjoying every bite.

Dinner Out

Fast-Food Frenzy

Most fast food is loaded with fats and oils. Here's how to make it more healthy:

- Pick a sandwich with meat that's grilled instead of breaded or fried.
- Order whole wheat bread if it's available.
- Load veggies onto your sandwich or pizza.
- Order a side salad instead of fries or, if you crave fries, share them with a friend.
- Drink water or milk. If you're a shake or soda lover, order the smallest size.
- Don't "super-size" anything. Period.

In Your Face

You're watching TV, and an ad comes on for fast food. Does your mouth water, even though dinner is hours away? Be aware of how ads affect you. It's up to you to flip the channel and make the smart choice.

At a Sit-Down Restaurant

Take advantage of the choices on the menu:

- Look for a meal that includes all of the food groups.
- Choose a baked potato instead of fries.
- Load up at the salad bar with dark green lettuce and lots of red, orange, and yellow veggies.
- Eat the lettuce and tomato garnish on your plate. Those pretty decorations are pretty good for you, too!

Size Wise

Most restaurants serve way more food than even an adult needs. Before you order, peek at what other customers have been served. Do the portions look large? Ask for a half order, or split a meal with someone else. Or scoop half of your meal into a take-home container to enjoy later on.

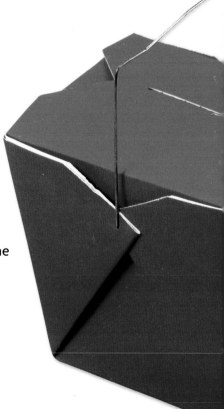

Snack Attack

Fruits and Veggies First

Dip sliced apples in yogurt for a sweet treat. Or slide fruit and cheese on a skewer to make a fruit kabob. Store cut-up vegetables in the fridge with a little water so that they stay crisp. To dress them up, dip them in peanut butter or low-fat ranch dressing. Frozen peas and fresh snap peas make great snacks, too.

Salty Snacks

Grab a handful of whole-grain cereal, or mix it with nuts and raisins for a sweet and salty snack. Ask your parents if you can try baked chips or crackers—they have much less fat. Pack a handful in a small plastic bag rather than digging into the big bag. To add protein, layer crackers with cheese or peanut butter.

Trick Your Taste Buds

Everyone eats junk food now and then, and that's O.K. But when you can, try these snack substitutes:

If you're craving crunchy chips, try . . .

pretzels or a handful of roasted almonds.

If you're craving sweets or candy, try . . .

dried fruit, such as raisins or apricots.

If you're craving French fries, try . . .

popcorn sprinkled with Parmesan cheese.

If you're craving ice cream, try . . .

low-fat frozen yogurt.

If you're craving a milk shake, try . . .

a smoothie made with yogurt, ice, and fresh fruit.

Girl Picks

Instead of grabbing an ice pop, just freeze your favorite fruit juice. It's really fun trying to create tasty things.

Spread peanut butter and nuts over a banana, or make your own trail mix of nuts, dried fruit, and cereal.

Try frozen grapes. They taste like ice cream or sherbet!

Make nachos in the microwave! Grate some cheese and sprinkle it on top of chips. Have a parent microwave them until the cheese melts. Top the chips with salsa, fresh tomatoes, salad, anything. Yum!

Make a Saturday, which is like a sundae but healthier. Put some yogurt in a cup, and then blueberries, and then more yogurt, and then raspberries, and then more yogurt, and then a cherry on top!

Make strawberry soup! Ask a parent to cut up strawberries and put them into a bowl. Then pour some milk in. You can add a little sugar to make it sweeter, but it's good without.

Scoop the yogurt out of a small container. Put peanut butter around the edges of container, and put the yogurt back in. Place a popsicle stick in the yogurt, and freeze the container for 1 to 2 hours to make a peanutty popsicle!

Labels & Lists

1. Look at the serving size.

The information on the label is based on one serving of the snack, not the whole bag or box.

2. Check out the calories.

The higher the calories, the more likely they are to come from fats or sugar. Most girls your age need 1600 to 2000 calories per day. If too many come from unhealthy foods, your body may not be getting the nutrients it needs.

3. Scan the ingredients list.

The first one is the main ingredient, so watch out if sugar tops the list. Look for whole grains, too, which are better for you than white flour.

A Healthy Snack
(cereal)

Nutrition Facts

Serving Size 1 cup (27g)
Servings Per Container 10

Amount Per Serving

Calories 100   Calories from Fat 15

	% Daily Value
Total Fat 1.5g	2%
Saturated Fat 0g	0%
Trans Fat 0mg	0%
Cholesterol 0mg	0%
Sodium 190mg	8%
Potassium 170mg	5%
Total Carbohydrate 20g	2%
Dietary Fiber 4g	20%
Sugars 1g	
Protein 0g	

	% Daily Value
Protein	0%
Vitamin A	10%
Vitamin C	10%
Calcium	10%
Iron	45%
Vitamin D	10%
Thiamin	25%
Riboflavin	25%
Niacin	25%
Vitamin B6	25%
Folic Acid	50%
Vitamin B12	25%
Phosphorus	10%
Magnesium	10%
Zinc	25%
Copper	2%

INGREDIENTS: WHOLE GRAIN OATS,
MODIFIED CORNSTARCH, SUGAR, OAT BRAN,
SALT, CALCIUM CARBONATE, OAT FIBER,
CORNSTARCH, WHEAT STARCH, VITAMINS

Compare the labels of a healthy snack and a not-so-healthy snack.

A Not-So-Healthy Snack
(French fries)

Nutrition Facts

Serving Size 4 ounces (114g)
Servings Per Container 1

Amount Per Serving

Calories 380   Calories from Fat 180

% Daily Value

Total Fat 20g	31%
Saturated Fat 4g	20%
Trans Fat 0mg	5%
Cholesterol 0mg	0%
Sodium 220mg	9%
Potassium 170mg	5%
Total Carbohydrate 47g	16%
Dietary Fiber 5g	19%
Sugars 0g	
Protein 4g	

% Daily Value

Protein	0%
Vitamin A	0%
Vitamin C	10%
Calcium	2%
Iron	6%
Vitamin D	0%
Thiamin	0%
Riboflavin	0%
Niacin	0%
Vitamin B6	0%
Folic Acid	0%
Vitamin B12	0%
Phosphorus	0%
Magnesium	0%
Zinc	0%
Copper	0%

INGREDIENTS: POTATO, OIL

4. Look at the % daily value (DV) numbers. Healthy foods have a large amount (20% DV or more) of vitamins, minerals, and fiber and a small amount (less than 5% DV) of saturated fat and cholesterol. Healthy foods also go easy on *sodium*, or salt (less than 20% DV).

Don't Over-Read

Knowing how to read a label is helpful when you're checking out new foods or choosing between snacks. Reading labels all the time, though, can make you worry too much about numbers. Focus more on enjoying a variety of healthy foods than on reading the fine print.

Listen Up

Hunger Pains

The next time you're hungry, listen to your body. Is your stomach gurgling? Is your mouth watering? Do you feel a little tired? Take a minute to think about how hunger feels. That way you'll recognize it when it strikes again.

Feeling Full

Do you sometimes not know you're full until *after* you've stopped eating? That's because it takes a while for your brain to get the message from your stomach. Help your brain catch up by eating slowly. You'll feel best if you don't eat more—or less—than your body needs.

Mood & Food

It's easy to confuse hunger with other feelings, such as boredom or anxiety. If you don't feel physical signs of hunger, try to figure out what you *really* need.

If you're frustrated . . .

take a break. Go for a walk, or dance like crazy to an upbeat song.

If you're angry . . .

take three deep breaths. Then call a friend, or sort out your feelings by writing in a journal.

Are you hungry for food or for something else? Your body will let you know.

If you're bored . . .

find something to do with your hands, such as painting your toenails or beading a friendship bracelet.

If you're anxious . . .

turn on relaxing music, and take a warm bath. Or snuggle with your favorite pet—real or plush.

On the Move

Get your body moving for a total of 60 minutes a day. You'll build strong muscles, a sharp mind, and the confidence to tackle new challenges.

25 Ways to Get Moving

Make the most of recess.

1. Have a jump-rope marathon.
2. Race a friend around the playground.
3. Map out an obstacle course on the playground equipment.
4. Hop across a hopscotch board.
5. Play Freeze Tag or Capture the Flag or Four Square.

Make money and build muscle.

6. Rake leaves for your neighbors.
7. Shovel snow from driveways and sidewalks.
8. Wash windows (that you can reach without a ladder).
9. Organize a car wash.
10. Weed gardens and flower beds.

Use your imagination.

11. Pretend that you're a world-famous athlete getting ready for a big game or event.

12. Dance as if you're trying out for a music video.

13. Act like an instructor in a workout DVD.

14. Run as if you're an animal racing through the jungle or forest or desert.

15. Imagine that you're a gymnast performing in the Olympics.

Surprise your parents.

16. Walk the dog.

17. Clean your room as fast as you can.

18. Vacuum the house.

19. Carry in the groceries.

20. Take out the trash.

Have fun with friends.

21. Make up a dance routine and perform it for your parents.

22. Host a mini Olympics with made-up categories, such as hula-hooping and balloon ball.

23. Ask a parent if you and a friend can walk around the mall two or three times without stopping to shop.

24. Give piggyback rides and pushes on the swings to little kids in your neighborhood.

25. Go swimming or sledding or bike riding or in-line skating. EVERYTHING is more fun with friends!

Cool Tools

Want to make moving your body even more fun? Use a stopwatch to time yourself racing through an obstacle course. Another tool that every active girl needs is a water bottle. Your body loses water when you sweat. Drink a little before, during, and especially after exercise.

Girls on the Go

My friends and I make whirlpools by swimming in one direction for a while and then swimming the other way. It's hard work but lots of fun.

When my sister and I are watching TV and the commercials come on, we run around the yard as fast as we can and run back in before the commercials end.

Invite some friends over and laugh together. Believe it or not, laughing is really good for your body!

Here's advice from girls on staying fit and having fun.

Whenever my best friend comes over, I teach her gymnastics and she teaches me the things she learns in dance class. It's a great way to have fun and exercise too.

Think of an event that you're working on in history class. Now make up a cheer about it, with lots of jumps and kicks. You'll remember your facts and get your blood pumping.

Make a big hopscotch board with chalk. In each square, write an exercise, such as 5 push-ups. Grab a friend and play hopscotch. Toss a rock into a square, hop to it, and then do the exercise!

Make a cool obstacle course with chalk or cones. Grab a basketball, a hula hoop, or a jump rope. Dribble, hula, or jump through all the ups and downs you made for yourself!

Get friends together and make your own workout video! You can act goofy and still get exercise.

Dear American Girl,
My mom is always telling me
I need t...

American Girl
8400 Fairway Place
Middleton, WI 53562

...eep. What
should I do? —Helpless

What else do girls want to know about eating right and exercise? Read on to find out. If you have other questions, ask a parent or your doctor. The more you learn, the healthier you'll be.

Food & Fitness

I am a really picky eater. My mom gets frustrated sometimes because I don't like a lot of meals. What should I do? —Confused

Work with your mom to find foods that you *do* like. Go with her to the grocery store and look for something you'd like to try. Help her cook a new recipe. If you try a few bites and don't like it, don't make a big deal out of it. Have an extra helping of something you do like, or make a sandwich for yourself. Remember that tastes change, and stay open to trying the food again in a few months.

My mom is always telling me I need to exercise. I don't have any time after school because of homework. If I wake up early, Mom tells me to go back to sleep. What should I do? —Helpless

An hour of exercise might seem hard to fit into a day, but you don't have to do it all at once. Break it down into shorter bursts of exercise. Can you play a game of tag over recess? Dance in your room for 10 minutes before home-work? Take a 20-minute walk after dinner? Make the most of your time on weekends, and brainstorm with your mom to find activities that get your whole family moving.

Stuck in a food rut? No time to exercise? You're not alone!

I'm a junk-food junkie! I'm always too tired to do anything. I know it's because of the junk food, but it seems as if there is no good healthy food out there!
—Munched Out

Ask your parents to help you cut down on the junk food in the house. If it's not there, you'll be more likely to reach for something healthy. Next, find good foods that satisfy your cravings for junk food. Are you longing for potato chips? Try munching on nuts or pretzels. Thirsting for a soda? Try fizzy water mixed with a little fruit juice. Experiment until you find foods that taste just as good as they are good for you.

Special Diets

I am allergic to a lot of things. I feel left out when my friends want to do something that I can't do, like go out for ice cream. My allergies are limiting my life.
—Left Out

It's time to get creative about what you *can* eat. If you can't have ice cream, ask your doctor if you can eat frozen tofu or soy products. If you can't eat wheat, can you make pizza on rye crackers? Make your own snack to take along when your friends go out for food, or invite them to a restaurant that has options for you. You may not eat the same things, but you won't miss out on the fun of being together.

I'm a vegetarian. When I go to a friend's house to eat, sometimes they have meat in the meal. I don't want to be rude, but I don't want to eat the meat.
—Mixed Feelings

Let your friends and their parents know that you are vegetarian *before* you go to their house for a meal. Tell them what you eat and what you don't eat. Offer to bring your own main course. If they forget and prepare something with meat, politely skip that dish. Look for other things at the table that you can eat, and round out your meal with healthy snacks when you get home.

Cutting out certain foods doesn't have to mean missing out on all the fun.

I have braces. My friends always eat candy that I can't eat right in front of me. My mouth waters when I see it. What should I do? — Brace Face

Your braces are doing more than straightening your teeth. They're also helping you steer clear of foods that aren't that good for you. Which snack foods does your orthodontist say are O.K. to eat? Fill small bags with your favorites, and have them handy when others are eating things you can't. Focus on how your teeth will look when those braces come off. Your smile will be bright, and your body will be healthy, too.

Body Talk

I'm skinny, and I hate it! Everyone's always saying, "You look like a toothpick! Do you eat?" Of course I eat! I'm sick of people making fun of me.
—Sick of Being Skinny

Let your close friends know that you're tired of the same old remarks. Shrug off comments from other people by saying, "It's just the way I am," or "I guess it's my genes," which is probably true. Basic body shape is something you're born with. Some naturally thin girls fill out as they get older, but don't try to make yourself something you're not. If your doctor says your weight is O.K., don't worry about it. Focus on being strong and healthy.

Everybody, and every body, is unique. Here's what girls have to say about their own.

I am the tallest one in my class, and I am heavier than some of my friends. When they ask me how much I weigh, I am afraid to tell them. Please help!
—Heavier

To be healthy, a girl who is tall has to be heavier than her shorter friends. A five-foot-tall girl is likely to weigh about 30 pounds more than a girl who is a foot shorter. You can explain that to your friends, or you can keep your weight to yourself. Sometimes girls get way too hung up on numbers, and it's best to change the subject. The important thing is to know that your weight is normal. Stand tall and be proud of your height—it's part of what makes you unique.

Diet Dangers

I think I am way overweight. I keep trying to go on diets and lose some of the weight, but diets don't work for me. People don't call me names or anything. I just want to do this for myself. —Ready for a Change

It's great that you want to be at a healthy weight, but don't buy into the idea that you don't look "right" just the way you are. Your health is what matters most, and that's the best reason for trying to change your weight. Ask your doctor if you are in a healthy weight range. If he or she says you are too heavy, work together to set weight and fitness goals. Don't go it alone when it comes to dieting. You've already learned that many diets don't work, and some are even dangerous. A doctor or dietician can help you change your eating and exercise habits slowly and safely.

One of my friends is very skinny. Lately she's been throwing away most of her lunch. I'm worried that she might be anorexic, but I don't know what to do. Please help! —Fearful Friend

You're right to be concerned. Eating disorders such as anorexia and bulimia can cause serious harm to the body, or even death. A person with *anorexia* thinks she is fat when she isn't, and she starves herself or overexercises to be thin. A person with *bulimia* may overeat and then try to make up for it by throwing up or using laxatives. Tell an adult about your friend *immediately*. Talk to your parents, a teacher, or a school counselor. Your friend may be upset with you, but be patient and stand by her. You're doing the right thing. When she is healthy again, she'll know that you spoke up because you cared about her.

Sound a Little Like You?

If you think you may be too focused on food or your weight, talk to an adult that you trust—a parent, a doctor, a teacher, your school counselor, or a dietician. Don't keep your worries about weight to yourself. Eating disorders can quickly take control of your life. People who care about you and understand food issues can help you fight back.

4 Keys to
Confidence

1. Choose your friends wisely.

Can you think of a friend who has a healthy attitude about food and her body? Check off what's true about her:

- ❏ She eats regular meals, including breakfast.
- ❏ She eats healthy snacks but lets herself eat a little junk food now and then, too.
- ❏ She likes to be active and challenge her body.
- ❏ She seems to like the way she looks, even if her body isn't perfect.
- ❏ She encourages you to like yourself, too.

If your friend scored a 4 or 5, hang on to her. Surround yourself with people who are happy with themselves and aren't trying to be like someone else. You'll feel happier and more confident, too.

2. Look for healthy role models.

Is there someone who you think is beautiful who doesn't look like a supermodel? Maybe it's a teacher, an aunt, or an athlete whose body is strong, not skinny. When you hang up a photo of a celebrity, take a second look. Does she seem to respect herself and take care of her body? Don't clutter your walls—and your mind—with unhealthy images.

3. Be as kind to yourself as you are to your friends.

Before you criticize yourself, ask, "Would I say that to a friend?" Pay yourself compliments, and express your own style with clothing that's right for your body instead of following the latest fashion craze. Ignore supermodels and be a role model, a girl *other* girls want to hang around.

4. Give your body what it needs.

When you feel good physically, you feel good emotionally. Think about it—when you're sick, tired, or hungry, you feel crabby. It works the other way around, too. If you give your body the food, rest, and exercise it needs, you'll feel healthier and happier. Want to greet tomorrow with more confidence? Take care of your body today.

Write to us!
Tell us which food and
fitness tips you liked best.

Send your thoughts to:
Food & You Editor
American Girl
8400 Fairway Place
Middleton, WI 53562

(All comments and suggestions received
by American Girl may be used without
compensation or acknowledgment.
Sorry—photos can't be returned.)

Here are some other American Girl books you might like:

❑ I read it.

❑ I read it.

❑ I read it.

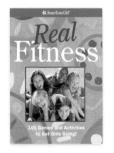

❑ I read it.

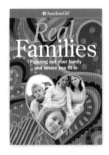

❑ I read it.

❑ I read it.